TURTLE POWER!

THE TEENAGE MUTANT NINJA TURTLES
The Unauthorized History

PROFILES • CLOTHING • REVIEWS
• MERCHANDISE • TRIVIA • ETC.

Publications International, Ltd.

Teenage Mutant Ninja Turtles® is a registered trademark of Mirage Studios U.S.A. Characters created by Kevin Eastman and Peter Laird. This publication was not created or licensed by, nor is Consumer Guide® or Publications International, Ltd. affiliated with, Mirage Studios U.S.A., New Line Cinema, Northshore Investments Limited, or Kevin Eastman and Peter Laird.

Unless otherwise noted, all characterizations and information relate to videos, cartoons, and the motion picture rather than to original comic characters.

PICTURE CREDITS

Family Home Entertainment: 4, 43, 44; **Sam Griffith Photography:** 5, 6, 9, 10, 13, 16, 18, 20, 21, 22, 23, 24, 25, 26, 27, 28, 29, 30, 31, 32, 33, 47, 48, 50, 51; **Group W Productions:** 59; **Alan Markfield/Shooting Star:** 17, 38, 39 (left), 40; **New Line Cinema Corp.:** 8, 12, 19, 37, 39 (right), 41, 62; **Chip Simons/New Line Cinema Corp.:** 14, 35; **Timothy White/Onyx:** 11, 63

Teenage Mutant Ninja Turtles® is a registered trademark of Mirage Studios U.S.A. Leonardo™, Michaelangelo™, Raphael™, Donatello™, Splinter™, April O'Neil™, Casey Jones™, Ace Duck™, Genghis Frog™, Metalhead™, Wingnut™ & Screwloose™, Shredder™, Foot Soldier™, Krang™, Baxter Stockman™, Rocksteady™, Bebop™, Rat King™, General Traag™, Turtle Blimp™, Sewer Playset™, and Retromutagen Ooze™ are trademarks of Mirage Studios U.S.A. Usagi Yojimbo™ is a trademark of Stan Sakai. Action figures and toys manufactured by Playmate Toys, Inc. Exclusively licensed by Surge Licensing, Inc.

Teenage Mutant Ninja Turtles is a registered trademark of Ultra Software Corporation/Konami Industry Co., copyright 1988. Nintendo® is a registered trademark of Nintendo of America Inc.

Barbie® and Masters of the Universe® are registered trademarks of Mattel, Inc. G.I. Joe® is a registered trademark of Hasbro, Inc. Mello Smello™ is a trademark of Mello Smello. Pizza Hut® is a registered trademark of Pizza Hut, Inc.

Heroes in a Half Shell™; Cowabunga, Shredhead; Hot Rodding Teenagers; The Shredder is Splintered; Incredible Shrinking Turtles; Case of the Killer Pizzas; and *Super Rocksteady and Mighty Bebop* are produced by Murakami Wolf Swenson, Inc., and distributed by Family Home Entertainment®, a registered trademark of International Video Entertainment Inc., a subsidiary of LIVE Entertainment Inc. *Teenage Mutant Ninja Turtles: The Storybook Based on the Movie* is published by Random House, Inc., New York. Motion picture copyright 1990 by Northshore Investments Limited.

Gift wrap set made by Unique Industries, Inc. Roller skates made by Brookfield Athletic Shoe Co., a subsidiary of Hyde Athletic Industries, Inc. Slippers made for Angel-etts of California. T-shirt made by Hugger.

CONTENTS

THE TURTLES STORY

hey love pizza! They fight crime! And they're GREEN! They're the Teenage Mutant Ninja Turtles, four very happening dudes who grew up in the sewers of New York City. Down in the slimy darkness of the sewers, four little turtles were exposed to some green ooze that was a powerful mutagen. Because of it, they changed into big, powerful teenage turtles. And they are experts in the art of the ninja. Radical, man!

Now, the Turtles are everywhere—in comics and cartoons, in videos and computer games, and in toy stores all across the country. But

When the Turtles come out of their sewer, they're ready to practice their ninja skills.

4

these mean, green, fighting machines are also becoming famous around the world, because *Teenage Mutant Ninja Turtles* is now a movie that has made more than 100 million greenbacks.

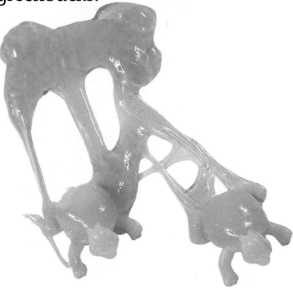

Two toy turtles are trying to escape from Retromutagen Ooze, the play version of the stuff that mutated the Turtles.

There are two legends about the origins of the Turtles and their ninja master, Splinter. In the cartoons and videos, Splinter used to be a wise old Japanese ninja master named Hamato Yoshi. He was betrayed by his evil disciple, Oroku Saki. Oroku took over Hamato Yoshi's Foot Clan and turned it into an evil force. He then became known as the Shredder. Yoshi was forced to flee to New York and live in the sewers. One day, a boy holding a bowl of pet turtles tripped and fell, and the turtles fell into the sewer. Yoshi found the turtles and took care of them. The Shredder poured a disgusting bright green gunk into the sewer over Yoshi, and some of it got on the turtles, too. Yoshi grew into the giant talking rat, Splinter, and the four turtles mutated into intelligent, teenage reptiles.

According to the comics created by Kevin Eastman and Peter Laird and the movie, *Teenage Mutant Ninja Turtles*, Splinter was not Hamato Yoshi himself, but his pet rat. The pet rat had learned the art of the ninja by watching his master. Yoshi and Splinter were forced to move to New York, where Splinter found himself without a home. One day, a truck swerved, and a canister fell out of it. The canister hit a bowl of turtles that a boy was carrying—and the canister and the bowl of turtles

Action figures show Master Splinter giving advice to the Ninja Turtles he has raised.

fell into a manhole. The canister broke open, and the glowing green ooze inside covered the turtles. Splinter picked up the turtles and got some of the ooze on himself, too.

In both versions, Splinter sees that the turtles have grown into intelligent adolescent turtles, so he teaches them the art of the ninja. He names them after famous artists of the Italian Renaissance—Michaelangelo, Raphael, Donatello, and Leonardo.

The Turtles legend owes a lot to other comic-book lore, because Eastman and Laird were comics fans. A Marvel Comics hero named Daredevil, for instance, is a blind acrobat who learned the secrets of *ninjutsu* from a master named Stick. He fought a band of evil ninja warriors called the Hand. So Eastman and Laird called their master Splinter and named his enemies the Foot.

The four tortoises are so popular because they don't try to be superheroes. They act like any other teenage hip dudes—they just know how to have a good time. They know how to kick shell, but they never attack first. Watch out, Superman! Move over, Batman! Here come the Teenage Mutant Ninja Turtles!

Cowabunga!

HARD-SHELL HEROES

hese are not your ordinary reptiles. They may come from different pet shops, but all four turtles shared the same slimy goo that made them mutants. Like the Musketeers, the Turtles are all for one and one for all. They love freedom and hate crime. They all love pizza, but they hate anchovies. They all wear face masks—they take them off only while sleeping. Each face mask is a different color. And each turtle has a weapon that is special to him. And he never carries just one. He's a cool guy—he always carries two!

The Ninja Turtles all love Splinter, who is like a good, wise dad to them, and he loves them, too. He makes the Turtles train in the martial arts, because he knows they'll need to fend for themselves in the mean streets of the Big Apple. But these Turtle heroes act like teenagers. And that means they get under each other's shell once in a while. Of course, they're the best of pals, so they always make up. There's usually some mega-move they have to make, like saving a pretty girl—April O'Neil—in distress.

MICHAELANGELO

Probably the most popular Turtle is Michaelangelo, known to his close pals as Mike. He's the joke-lover, the dude who never gets tired of a good prank or a good laugh.

This far-out hero likes to show off with his whirling *nunchukus*. These are two wooden sticks attached by a chain. They go, "Whak! Whak!" when this cool warrior twirls them in the air.

Mike is no simple warrior. He's the kind of shell-shocker who likes to fight with his favorite weapon in one hand and a slice of pizza in the other. This is the original pizza freak. He likes to call himself "master of the whirling pizzas."

He's a rock-'n'-rolling dude who will never pay full price for

Mike is the Turtle with the orange face mask and the whirling *nunchukus*.

cold pizza. He loves pizza too much! And the crazier the topping, the better. He falls head over heels for a good pickled-herring pizza with caramel topping. Or get a load of another Michaelangelo special—marshmallow and asparagus topping. Totally delicioso, man! How about that for a gourmet mutant?

Mike cracks a joke a minute, even when he's busy 'chukking.

What would you expect from a rude and crude surfer dude? He's a real party animal, and he knows how to have a good time even when the times are slow. Nobody can do a meaner imitation than Michaelangelo. He can do Sylvester Stallone as Rocky, and he can wipe you out with his James Cagney routine. Mike knows plenty about these people, because he watches turtlevision.

Mark Freedman, who is in charge of licensing all the Turtles action figures and other toys, told *Newsday* that Michaelangelo is like Spicoli, the far-out teenager in the comedy *Fast Times at Ridgemont High*. His

Face mask: Orange
Weapon: Nunchukus
Birthplace: Woody's Pet Shop, Pennshellvania
Height: 5 feet
Weight: 150 pounds
Age: 15 ½ people years

life in the movie was one long party. That sounds just like our green, mean, pizza-gobbling machine!

Even in the middle of an all-out battle against the bad guys, Mike won't get serious. He's always looking for the light side. The fearsome foursome may be peeling rubber some of the time, but Mike is always chilled out enough to come up with something funny.

Mike's the fun-loving Turtle. This action figure shows him break dancing with his weapon ready.

An example is the video *Super Rocksteady and Mighty Bebop.* The Shredder has zombified a bunch of humans. Our wild and crazy tortoise gets a rush out of hearing them chant, "You command, we obey! You command, we obey!" Mike finds the rhythm catchy. Not that he doesn't care about the Shredder's victims. He is on his way to save them. But that's his way of cheering his crime-fighting pals—and himself, too.

Sometimes, Mike can be so easygoing that he underestimates an opponent. And on some mornings, he can get radically impatient when the Turtles do their ninja training. If you think about pizza all day long, you might forget about the job! But his pals are there to remind him that anchovies aren't his biggest enemy. The Shredder and the Foot Clan are always lurking in the shadows with some evil plot on their minds. At the right moment, Mike swings on a rope like Tarzan or jumps into action from a Turtle Blimp.

Even the toy Michaelangelo loves his pizza—but no anchovies, please!

But Mike is not just a goofy, happy-go-lucky dude. He has a heart, too. In the video *Enter the Fly,* when April faints and looks as though she's dead, Mike's the first to worry about her.

Master Splinter named this super party animal after Michelangelo, the famous Italian painter, sculptor, and architect of the Renaissance period. Michelangelo lived in the fifteenth century. He made the famous sculptures "David," "Moses," and "Pieta." He also painted the ceiling of the Sistine Chapel, in Vatican City, with a beautiful scene of the Creation.

DONATELLO

Donatello's the smart Turtle—he's a whiz at mechanics.

O f all the Ninja Turtles, Donatello is the brainiest under the shell. Sometimes called Don by his reptile friends, he is a quiet, thoughtful dude. You can always grab Don's attention by showing him a good gadget or a book. He knows all there is to know about machines. When they break down, nobody can fix them better than he can. If it's a computer, he can handle it. If it's a broken weapon, no problemo!

Don invented turtlevision all by himself. He put together discarded odds and ends and came up with a radical idea. He also invented the turtle communicator. This invention helps our heroes keep in touch with each other—and with their friends, too.

And the Turtle Van—Don designed that! The Turtle Blimp, too. This dynamite dude doesn't have to worry about spare parts. He'll make them himself. And then he'll grab a play by Shakespeare.

Don may be a thinker, but when he comes out of the sewer, he's ready for action.

But this cool Turtle isn't all brains. Just check out his muscles! And he can really fight. His favorite weapon is the *bo,* a big staff that he wields with gusto against his enemies.

Because Don is bright, he can really think on the spot. When he doesn't have a plan of action, he invents one. In the video *The Mutagen Monster,* a mad, "moo-tant" giant bull is threatening Donatello's green pals. Don uses a crane on a construction site as a device to lasso the bull. Don's never short of ideas.

His great scientific mind sometimes tells him when some mega-trouble is brewing. In *The Mutagen Monster,* a train collision causes a major spill of chemicals. In a situation like that, less awesome dudes would simply haul shell. Don knows there's going to be trouble, and he's ready for it.

This tortoise has a very strong sense of self. He's proud to be a Turtle—and a Mutant Ninja one at that! In the video *Super Rocksteady and Mighty Bebop,* he informs April's boss, the TV station manager, "Turtles are not slime!"

It's not that he gets insulted easily. No way! He has an outstanding sense of humor. In the movie *Teenage Mutant Ninja Turtles,* he has a lot of fun exchanging insults with Casey Jones, the guy who helps our mean, green heroes fight crime. "Fungoid," Casey calls him. "Gackface!" Don snaps back.

In the movie, he also shows that he can be quite emotional. Leonardo takes care of the wounded Raphael, and they put their arms around each other like true pals and brothers. That

Face mask: Purple
Weapon: Bo
Birthplace: Joe's Pet Place, Slowklahoma
Height: 4 feet
Weight: 145 pounds
Age: 15 people years

moves Don plenty. "I guess I'm just a sentimental fool!" he says, sniffling.

According to Mark Freedman, who's a major Turtles expert, Donatello is brainy, like filmmaker and actor Woody Allen.

In the movie *Teenage Mutant Ninja Turtles,* Don's voice is that of teen idol Corey Feldman, from *Stand By Me* and *License to Drive.*

Donatello was named after Donatello, a famous sculptor from Florence, Italy. He was born in the fourteenth century, and his most famous statue is one of David.

Don's the Turtle with the purple face mask. His action figure comes with two of his weapon, the bo.

RAPHAEL

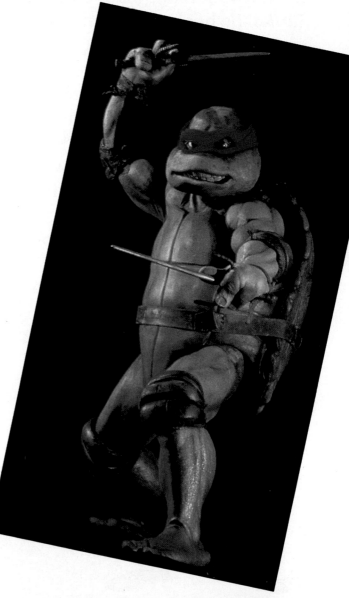

Raphael is the Ninja Turtle with the red-hot temper. Known to his green pals as Raph, this dude thinks he's really cool. But he sometimes needs chilling out.

Like Michaelangelo, he's rude and crude. And he has an attitude. But if you ask him about it, he'll come back with, "I have an attitude?" He's known as the "Snapping Ninja," the reptile who can snap with maximum sarcasm and simply wipe you out. He's quick to respond when you drive him out of his shell!

But don't think this reptile is good only at snapping. He is even better at using his favorite weapon, a three-pronged dagger called a *sai*. It goes, "Whak! Sptang! Chtak!" He knows how

Raph is the Turtle with the red face mask. With a sai in each hand, he can face danger.

to throw his dagger high and far, and he can hit a target from an awesome distance! He sends it flying through the air to destroy the dangerous, powerful Mesmerizer—the evil hypnotizing machine used by the Shredder to gain control over the city.

And if he doesn't totally trash the bad guys with his *sai*, you can bet your shiny shell he's going to make a move with a heavy manhole cover. That should flatten the slimy Foot Clan, at least for a while!

Raphael is a shrewd dude who knows the ins and outs of tactical warfare. He understands that sometimes it's better to cut off the enemy's line of supply than to try to trash him totally up front. This mean, green fighting machine is a brave one. And he always dares the enemy to attack. Does he ever get cold feet? No way!

This naughty Ninja is some kind of rebel. That means that he sometimes prefers working alone to being part of a team. But he can show more team spirit than you might think. In

Face mask: Red
Weapon: *Sai*
Birthplace: Shelly's Pet City, New Hampshell
Height: 5 feet, 1 inch
Weight: 147 pounds
Age: 15 people years

the video *Super Rocksteady and Mighty Bebop,* Raph traps those two bumbling mutants in a revolving door. He does this by throwing his *sai* after them when they try to get away. Then Leonardo gives the door a final touch—or spin. He makes them spin like a propeller out of control. When they put their shelly minds to it, these two Turtles work pretty well together.

Raph's the kind of tortoise who jumps first and looks later. He's a real hothead! And that can sometimes get a green teen into trouble. For example, in the video *The Mutagen Monster,* Raph gets into an awesome food fight with Michaelangelo. They argue

Raph may be able to take a beating, but this toy Raph is posed to dish one out, too.

about what program to watch on turtlevision, and they throw pizzas at each other instead of words.

But it's all fun and games. Raph never loses his sharp tongue, even when things get shelly. When he has to wipe out a bunch of evil robots in the video *Heroes in a Half Shell,* he does an outstanding job. But he also snaps at his metallic foes, "Where do these guys get their gear? Mars?" After that, he goes on to save April from drowning.

In the movie, *Teenage Mutant Ninja Turtles,* Raphael gets beaten up by the evil Foot when he's all alone on a rooftop. His Turtle buddies are busy in the sewer. When Raph returns home, badly hurt, you don't hear him say one word of complaint! This dude is no crybaby. He can take a beating and suffer in silence. Like a true-green ninja hero!

Raph is a reptile full of contradictions. He's witty but also serious. In the original comic book, Raph was a little bit crazy. He was a kind of spoof on a Marvel Comics character named Wolverine, who was also a hothead. Later, Eastman and Laird started making Raphael a little nicer.

In the movie, Raph is played by actor Josh Pais, a 31-year-old resident of New York. Josh paid a lot of attention to his favorite reptile. He told *New York* magazine, "Raphael is the most troubled turtle, the one with the most problems to work out."

Splinter named him after Raphael, the great Italian artist and architect of the Renaissance period. This artist specialized in religious paintings and designed churches and palaces. He was born five centuries ago.

LEONARDO

Leonardo is the unofficial leader of the green, shelly pack. Nicknamed Leo by his fellow troupers, he's the oldest of Master Splinter's disciples. And nobody is closer to the sage and wise rat. He will listen to Splinter when no one else will.

He's an excellent thinker and an awesome fighter. He's truly amazing with his weapon of choice, a long sword known as a *katana* blade. In the video *The Case of the Killer Pizzas,* Leo waves his sword like a true wizard and saves the day.

But that's not all. Give Leo a ninja star, and he'll total anybody who stands in his way. Give him *any* weapon, and he'll wield it like a real pro. He's not the leader for nothing!

Leonardo's the Turtle who is closest to Master Splinter.

But Leo is a serious Turtle, one who always thinks before he gets into something. He's careful, disciplined—like a true ninja—and he always keeps his cool in battle.

True to the teachings of Master Splinter, he always prefers to settle a dispute

With his blue face mask and his katana blades, the toy Leonardo is posed for a feat of bravery.

Face mask: Blue
Weapon: *Katana* blades
Birthplace: McMahon's Pet Emporium, Chesabeake Bay
Height: 5 feet, 1 inch
Weight: 155 pounds
Age: 16 people years

without using violence. In the video *New York's Shiniest,* Leo and his shiny-shelled gang save April from burglars without trashing the burglars.

He has a strong conscience. He always wants to do the right thing, to be a moral reptile. If he comes across someone in trouble, he's always willing to help him or her out—human, animal, or mutant.

He springs to action on the double to help anyone who needs it. In the video *The Mutagen Monster,* the cowardly Vernon, April's jealous partner at the TV station, grabs her camera and wants to get the scoop himself. But when Vernon sees the monster, he gets cold feet and runs away. Now, this kind of coward may not deserve any help. But Leonardo is a kind and brave fighter, and he convinces his pack to help Vernon.

You can count on Leo to initiate a rescue operation. He uses his wisdom to get his shelly pals ready for feats of glory. He can come up with pearls of

Leonardo knows that you sometimes have to fight evil in roundabout ways.

wisdom that Splinter himself would be proud of. For example, in the video *The Case of the Killer Pizzas,* Leo says, "Sometimes you have to make a pact with evil in order to fight evil." By that, he means that sometimes you can find yourself on the side of one evil force just so that you can defeat another, more vicious opponent. And afterward, of course, you go after the first evil, too.

In the movie, *Teenage Mutant Ninja Turtles,* when Splinter disappears and our four green teen heroes are at a loss, Leonardo saves the day. He goes by himself into the woods and spends long hours meditating with his eyes closed. He becomes fully concentrated. And then he hears Splinter's voice talking to him even though the master rat is not there. It's clear that when Splinter is not around, Leo can almost match his wisdom.

Leonardo is named after Leonardo da Vinci, one of the greatest geniuses of all time. He was a sculptor, an architect, an engineer, a painter, and a scientist. He was born in the fifteenth century. His most famous paintings are "Mona Lisa" and "The Last Supper."

TURTLE FRIENDS AND FOES

THE GOOD GUYS

Splinter

Splinter is the master ninja rat and the spiritual father of the four Turtles. He's a great martial arts expert, and he has great powers. He is too old to go out fighting against his mortal enemy, the Shredder, but he wisely teaches the Turtles to win. But sometimes Splinter joins a mission for the glory of it—or to save his pals! Since Splinter was born in Japan, he doesn't eat pizza—he enjoys *sushi*.

He's a firm believer in nonviolent means to resolve conflicts. Indeed, this kindly rat loves his disciples like sons. He shares his wisdom with them, but he never lectures or reproaches them. He sets an example.

The kindly ninja rat's action figure gives Splinter weapons in case he has to join in a mission.

Bobby Herbeck, who wrote the screenplay of the movie, *Teenage Mutant Ninja Turtles,* told *Comics Interview* that Splinter is like the wise karate master in *The Karate Kid.* He's a sage and a mentor to his young pupils.

The toy April wears a yellow jumpsuit like the cartoon April.

April O'Neil

In the videos and in the movie, April is an enterprising, pretty, and hip TV news reporter who joins the Turtles in their fight against crime. She's the station's star reporter, and she's eager and determined to follow every lead to get her story. But she often gets into trouble. Then, the Turtles come to her rescue.

The comic-book April isn't a reporter. Instead, April started out working as a computer programmer—and she worked for Baxter Stockman building

mousers. Even though her boss was nuts, April was still a good person. She quickly realized that Bax wasn't quite right in the head, and she tried to leave.

April is the only woman with an important role in the Turtle story. She's clever and brave and has a sensitive side, too. In the movie, *Teenage Mutant Ninja Turtles,* April is played by actress Judith Hoag. Judith told *Starlog,* "April is a very funny, very smart woman with a purpose. Her whole family has died and she has been left out there to do her thing and with a whole lot to prove to the world." Her favorite color is bright yellow. Her favorite team is green.

Casey Jones

Casey Jones had been a professional hockey player for a year, but he got hurt and had to quit. Then he found a whole new use for those hockey sticks of his. At night, Casey puts on his hockey mask and fills his backpack with all kinds of sports equipment. Then he goes around looking for people who

Casey Jones's action figure gives him a golf bag full of bats and sticks.

are committing crimes, and he beats them up with hockey sticks, baseball bats, cricket bats—even golf clubs. Casey is slightly crazy.

At first glance, he may seem tough, rude, and juvenile. But once you get to know him, he's sweet and good. No wonder April develops a soft spot for him, as he does for her. Steve Barron directed the movie, *Teenage Mutant Ninja Turtles.* In *Comics Interview,* he compares Casey to Han Solo in *Star Wars.* Barron calls him "a great

interesting character . . . like a roving pirate who became a good guy." The intense Casey is played by actor Elias Koteas in the movie. He first challenges the Turtles, then joins their team. This sports fan loves to crack jokes and, according to some, could use a good shower.

Ace Duck

Ace Conrad was a famous test pilot who had the bad luck to fly his plane into one of the Shredder's energy beams. But instead of having his goose cooked, Ace wound up as a duck.

Once Krang had a sudden craving for duck brain, so he told the Shredder to beam a

Huge yellow wings make the toy Ace Duck ready to fly.

duck to him in Dimension X. But when Ace flew into the beam, he fused with the duck—and Ace Duck was born. In the confusion Ace crashed into the sewer. Luckily, he wasn't hurt. Trying to find his way out, he wandered into the Turtles' headquarters and made friends. As a result, Leo, Mike, Raph, and Don decided to give Ace a job piloting their Turtle Blimp.

Since he's also a mutant, the toy Genghis Frog can stand upright.

Genghis Frog

Genghis Frog had a close encounter with some of the Shredder's mutagen. He was just a poor little tadpole when he accidentally ran into the stuff—but then, through the wonders of radiation, he became a five-foot-tall frog.

The Shredder tricked him into joining his band of mutants for a while. But it didn't take Gengy long to realize that the Shredder was pond scum, so he switched to the Turtles' side. Now he leads his fellow frogs—and helps the Turtles make the Shredder see green.

Metalhead

Enemy Krang wasn't having much luck against the green teens. So he decided that he needed a turtle to beat a Turtle. He built a robot version and sent

Metalhead's action figure serves up the Turtles' favorite snack.

it after our four tortoises. But Donatello, the clever dude, reprogrammed Metalhead to become the Turtles' butler. The robot makes a great housekeeper—and he can cook, too. He makes a great pepperoni and ice cream pizza.

Metalhead has also been programmed to play a great selection of rock 'n' roll—especially heavy metal.

Danny Pennington

Danny Pennington is a neglected kid in the movie, *Teenage Mutant Ninja Turtles*. This rebel is the 13-year-old son of Charles Pennington, April's boss at the TV station where she works. Danny, played by actor Michael Turney, is a lonely kid, because his dad doesn't pay attention to him. That's why he joins the Shredder's gang of teen ninja thieves. Then he tips his evil boss about the Turtles' hideout. This restless, impressionable kid later realizes his mistake and joins April, Casey, and the green teens in their fight against crime.

Usagi Yojimbo

Usagi Yojimbo was a *ronin*—a masterless *samurai* of ancient Japan. But he's a giant rabbit. A *samurai* is very honorable—and really good with a sword. Donatello's trans-dimensional portal accidentally pulled this *samurai* rabbit into the Turtles' world, and the result was a brawl. Splinter managed to calm things down—after the Turtles got their shells kicked—and convinced Yojimbo that they were the good guys.

The toy Usagi Yojimbo is a rabbit ronin *from his neatly tied ears down to his shoes.*

Wingnut's big bat wings are loaded with weapons on the toy figure. His friend Screwloose is by his side.

Wingnut and Screwloose

Wingnut is from a planet of vampire bats called Huanu. For a bloodsucker, it was a pretty nice place to live—until Krang blew it up. Wingnut and his mosquito buddy, Screwloose, survived the explosion. They were sucked into a whirlpool and blown all the way to Earth. They soon ran into the Turtles, who decided they were all right—even if they are bloodsuckers.

Wingy swore to get revenge on Krang for destroying his people. But he's a complete klutz, and he's got bats in his belfry. The Turtles have been trying to help him, but so far he can't avoid bumping into walls. His pal Screwloose has some sense, so maybe there's hope for Wingnut after all.

THE BAD GUYS

This toy figure of the Shredder shows an evil character with deadly blades on his arms and legs.

The Shredder

The Shredder is the bad guy you love to hate. His real name is Oroku Saki. He wears a mean-looking metal helmet and mask, which makes him look like Darth Vader in *Star Wars*. This Japanese-born villain, who once betrayed Hamato Yoshi, wants to achieve world domination. He knows how to get others to do his dirty work for him. He has gotten together the members of the Foot Clan, who obey his every command. This ruthless, vengeful monster is actually not

his own boss. He has to turn to Krang, the bodiless brain, for advice. That's because the Shredder himself is more evil than bright. He's always ready to destroy and cause pain and suffering for others. And that makes him the number one enemy of the Ninja Turtles. In the movie, the Shredder is played by actor James Saito.

Foot Soldier action figures are like the high-tech robots of the cartoons.

The Foot

The Foot Clan, who are the Shredder's evil soldiers, are portrayed in the cartoons as robots with high-tech weaponry. In the movie, *Teenage Mutant Ninja Turtles*, the Foot are human—young boys corrupted by the Shredder and Master Tatsu. They are a gang of thieves—like Fagin's trained pickpockets in *Oliver Twist*. They, too, are trained in *ninjutsu*. But even a crowd of them are no match for the Turtles.

Krang

Krang is pink, like a baby, but there's nothing sweet about him. This brain without a body has ugly-looking tentacles and sharp teeth. But he has to depend on others to carry out his vicious ideas. This pitiful monster wants to dominate the world. He must use the Shredder to do that—and even to find a body for him. This pile of goo is never satisfied with the Shredder's actions, and he's basically a big whiner. He's always ranting and raving. Krang hates anyone who has a good time, because he can't enjoy himself. This bumbling brain was born in Dimension X. He certainly should have stayed there!

The toy Krang is a gruesome pink brain sitting in a mechanical body.

Baxter Stockman's action figure shows the mad scientist transmutated into a fly.

Baxter Stockman

Baxter Stockman is a nerdy, spineless inventor who is terrorized by the Shredder into joining his evil schemes. He wears glasses, his hair is all over the place, and he wears a white scientist's apron. The Shredder never appreciates what this absent-minded professor tries to do for him. Baxter invents a Rat Catcher to trap Splinter—and what does he get in return? Cross-mutated with a fly—just like in the movie *The Fly*. A pat on the back would have been fine!

You can tell from Rocksteady's toy figurine just how stupid he is.

Rocksteady

Rocksteady was a gray rhino in the zoo until the Shredder cross-mutated him with a common hoodlum. He is so stupid he can't carry out the orders that his evil boss gives him. He's more stupid than evil, though. He is physically strong, and he doesn't mind serving a bad cause. The only sensitive things about this creature are his ears, which the Shredder

enjoys pulling on. And what does Rocksteady do? He complains a little, and then thanks his master!

Bebop

Before he met the Shredder and the evil Foot Clan, Bebop used to be your ordinary, run-of-the-mill warthog in the zoo. As if that weren't unattractive enough, he was cross-mutated with a very stupid hoodlum. This ugly brownish-pink mutant is Rocksteady's partner in mischief. And he's no less dumb and bumbling himself. He sports a purple Mohawk hairdo and wears purple shades and tennis

Bebop's action figure sports sunglasses and a purple Mohawk hairdo.

shoes, but that doesn't make him hip. He sometimes uses a garbage can lid as a shield, but that doesn't prevent him from getting clobbered by the Turtles. Because he's so dumb, he usually manages to mess up the Shredder's plans.

A mean expression on his ugly face, the toy General Traag strides off carrying his laser blaster.

Rats crawl all over the action figure of Rat King, and the hide of a cat hangs from his belt.

Rat King

Dressed in rags and playing a magic flute, Rat King is the Pied Piper gone nasty. He uses his flute to hypnotize mice into serving him. Not even Splinter can resist his power. Rat King and the Shredder are in a running war for the possession of the sewer—and the Turtles are caught in the middle.

General Traag

Based in Dimension X, General Traag is the vicious leader of Krang's Rock Soldier armies. This warrior is a laser weapons freak. And he uses them a lot when he comes to Earth to help his master fight the Turtles. He is a very powerful enemy of our lean, green fighting machines. He can penetrate a mountain of stone with his laser blaster, and the Turtles need all their ninja training to fend him off. This ugly-looking commander is not someone to take lightly. He is as fearsome as he is evil. Not someone you'd like to meet in a dark alley—or anywhere else!

HOW THE TURTLES BEGAN

The idea of the Teenage Mutant Ninja Turtles was born one autumn night in 1983 in Northampton, Massachusetts. Their creators were Kevin Eastman and Peter Laird. The two were having a hard time making a living in the field they loved—comic illustrations. Kevin even worked as a short-order cook to make a living.

On that autumn evening, Kevin and Peter were watching TV and just hanging out. They were in a creative mood. Kevin said to *The New York Times,* "For some reason, I came up with a sketch of a turtle with a mask. Pete did one and [then] another

The original Teenage Mutant Ninja Turtles comic book is now a collector's item worth around $300.

. . . . Then I drew four turtles, each with a different weapon. I said, 'Why not call them Ninja Turtles?' Pete said, 'Why not Teenage Mutant Ninja Turtles?'"

30

The two cartoonists didn't know they had given birth to a phenomenon. Kevin told the *Chicago Tribune,* "We laughed at it, chucked it aside and went to sleep." Still, they soon became enchanted enough with their invention to offer it to Marvel Comics. They were turned down, so they borrowed $700 from Kevin's uncle and added $500 of their own money to print 3000 copies of their first Turtles comic. The black-and-white comic appeared in April 1984 and was sold out. A second issue of 15,000 copies appeared six months later, and it too sold out.

"It was around issue three that we could actually pay our bills and keep us in macaroni and cheese," Kevin told the *Boston Globe.* "That was the dream come true: to actually make a living drawing something that we'd wanted to do since we could read comics." When the reptiles' adventures came out in color, their fans grew even more numerous.

Entrepreneur Mark Freedman met Kevin and Peter in 1986.

When the Turtles comics became a success, Eastman and Laird felt their dream had come true.

Since the comic books were so popular, Mark felt that the Turtles would make a good line of toys. "I did not create the Turtles," Mark told *Newsday,* "but I discovered them." By now, he has introduced hundreds of Turtles products and made the Turtles famous.

In association with Mirage Studios, which is owned by Kevin and Peter, Archie Comics now publishes a Turtles comic book—in color—every six weeks (half a million copies)!

After a highly successful five-part Turtles miniseries in 1987, the Turtles became the stars of a syndicated animated cartoon

Videos continue the cartoon adventures of the green teens.

series. The series helped our green teens find more and more fans, and younger ones, too.

That same year, Turtlesmania went video. There are seven videos starring our lean, mean fighting machines. They are *Cowabunga, Shredhead; Hot Rodding Teenagers; The Shredder is Splintered; Incredible Shrinking Turtles; Heroes in a Half Shell; Case of the Killer Pizzas;* and *Super Rocksteady and Mighty Bebop.* Most of these videos include more than one Turtles adventure.

Other companies joined the Turtles bandwagon. Burger King began offering four low-priced Turtles videos to its customers: *April Foolish, Invasion of the Turtle Snatchers, The Great Boldini,* and *Sky Turtles.* Needless to say,

many kids—200,000 daily— gobbled up their meals and took their videos home with them. And Nintendo has come up with a Turtles game for its entertainment system.

Perhaps the top achievement for the reptiles was becoming movie stars. Their full-length movie, *Teenage Mutant Ninja Turtles,* became one of the greatest hits of 1990, grossing more than $100 million. It has spawned a rap-music soundtrack that contains two hit singles, "Turtle Power" and "Spin That Wheel." A sequel to the movie is already planned, and producer David Chan told the *Los Angeles Times* that it will be "even more entertaining."

But that's not the end of it. This fall, the reptiles will join the

CBS Saturday morning lineup with 26 new Turtles cartoons. And the Turtles will be seen on stage during a 40-city tour that starts at New York's Radio City Music Hall in September 1990. Instead of showing off their ninja weapons, they will prove their musical talents and perform a rock concert. Mike will play the guitar, Don the keyboards, Leo the bass, and

Random House

The movie plot in book form is only one of the many Turtles adventures in books.

Raph the sax. This is not the same music featured in the movie. The show will have new songs, such as "No Need to Mutate" and "Pizza Power." The sponsor of the tour is Pizza Hut.

The Turtles have also made appearances on the printed page. *Teenage Mutant Ninja Turtles: The Storybook Based on the Movie* is currently available. Another book, *Teenage Mutant Ninja Turtles: The First Battle,* illustrated by Larry Daste, has become a best-seller.

Our green friends are showing up everywhere. Action figures, coloring books, and hundreds of merchandising tie-ins have appeared for Turtles lovers of all ages.

But the influence of the Turtles goes beyond their books and merchandising. Their popularity seems endless. In the farewell episode of the TV series *Magnum, P.I.,* actor Tom Selleck is shown reading a *Teenage Mutant Ninja Turtles* comic book. The Pittsburgh Pirates consider the Turtles their inspiration. The Pirate clubhouse is full of Turtles posters, and team members speak to each other in the reptiles' favorite expressions.

In May 1990, a Mutant Ninja Turtle Day was proclaimed in Massachusetts. Representative William Nagle from the town of Northampton—where the reptiles were created—told the *Boston Globe,* "We've given the world Calvin Coolidge, the graham cracker, and Teenage Mutant Ninja Turtles."

Why are the Turtles so popular? They stir the imagination, they are funny, and they're kids themselves!

Some parents are not happy with the violence the reptiles are involved in. The National Coalition on Television Violence agrees. In the *Boston Globe,* that organization called the movie *Teenage Mutant Ninja Turtles* "a needless glorification of violence."

In England, the name of the series was changed to *Teenage Mutant Hero Turtles.* The word "Ninja" was taken out by the BBC because it refers to Japanese assassins. The cartoons were also recut to omit most of the violence.

By contrast, defenders of the Turtles claim that this kind of tongue-in-cheek action isn't harmful to kids. Others remind us that the Turtles are peaceful creatures that attack only when they are victimized by others. According to the martial arts philosophy, power should be used only when peaceful means to resolve the conflict have been used up.

Their co-creator, Peter Laird, told the Associated Press, "The Turtles live their lives with the philosophy that they don't want to hassle anybody and they don't want to be hassled themselves. But when trouble comes, they're able to handle it."

Actually, the early Turtles, drawn in black and white, were more violent. Their color adventures show them as friendlier—they smile a lot, they don't growl, and they don't actually kill anyone. They stand for the same principles, though.

Unlike Superman and Batman, the traditional comic-

The Turtles—and their friend April—are more fun-loving than other comic heroes.

book heroes who fight for justice and freedom, the Turtles are more tongue-in-cheek. They also don't possess such supernatural powers as flying through the air. In fact, Kevin Eastman and Peter Laird intended them to spoof the superheroes of comics. These green teens are supposed to be like other teenagers, though they're a bit more adept at getting out of trouble. While Batman has a dark side and Superman is not strong on humor, the Ninja Turtles are all about having fun. But they take time out from their fun to fight the bad guys.

The bad guys include those who sell and buy drugs. No wonder President Bush has recruited the Turtles to join his antidrug campaign. In his address to the Academy of Television Arts and Sciences, he praised the Turtles for their influence on children.

The martial arts have benefited from the reptiles, too. A karate studio owner in Nashville, Tennessee, hosts Teenage Mutant Ninja Turtles (TMNT) parties. In Washington, D.C., a martial arts studio advertised TMNT classes for all ages.

Furthermore, the Turtles seem to have an environmental point of view. For one thing, they're helping to save real-life turtles. A benefit screening of the movie held in Washington in March 1990 raised $10,000 for turtle aid. The Ninja Turtles' creators and the Center for Marine Conservation are discussing conservation-theme stories for the TV cartoon series. Perhaps the Turtles are a good example for teaching kids to care about all living things—people and animals alike.

THE TURTLES ON THE SCREEN

The Teenage Mutant Ninja Turtles are not the first comic-book heroes to become TV and movie stars. Superman and Batman had movies and television shows that were big hits. But Superman and Batman take themselves a lot more seriously. Their mission is to protect the world from evil influences. The Turtles aren't looking for trouble—but if trouble comes, they're ready. And the Turtles laugh and joke around—other superheroes are pretty humorless.

The movie *Teenage Mutant Ninja Turtles* is tremendously successful, but that's partly because kids already loved the Turtles. Kids had been watching Turtles cartoons and playing with Turtles action figures before the movie was made. But the green teens are not the first toy figures to become movie stars, either. In 1987, the movie *Masters of the Universe* showed characters on the screen that were very popular action figures and a TV series. But that movie was nowhere near as successful as *Teenage Mutant Ninja Turtles*.

You'd think that because the Turtles are so popular with kids, a movie about them would be a natural. But Thomas Gray, the person in charge of the production of the movie, nearly

Master puppeteer Jim Henson poses with Raph, Don, Mike, and Leo.

turned it down. Gray is an executive at Golden Harvest Films, a company that specializes in movies about martial arts. It wasn't until someone showed him a comic book that he wanted to make the movie.

Mark Freedman, the man in charge of marketing Turtles products, and Golden Harvest Films both agreed that a movie about the Turtles should not be animated. People could watch cartoons of the Turtles on television or in videos. They agreed that the movie should make the Turtles come alive.

The late Jim Henson, who created the Muppets, was hired to develop the Turtles and Splinter. It was a tall order, because the Turtles had to be completely free to roam around and interact with the human actors. They had to move quickly and talk like real teenagers. And they had to look like the Ninja Turtles everyone loved from the comics and cartoons.

The Turtles were played by actors wearing body casts made of latex. The body casts weighed 70 pounds. The raincoats the green teens wore on the streets of New York added 12 pounds to the burden. It took one and a half hours for the actor to get into his suit. For that reason, they had a backup team of Turtles in case one of the actors needed to get out of his suit. Waiting for him to get back into costume would cause a long delay in the shooting.

The Shredder's costume is the same as in the comics. Fans would be disappointed to see him any other way.

The man who first wore Raph's suit broke his nose in one of the early scenes and had to be replaced.

Actually, there were four teams of Turtles. In addition to the actors and their backups, there were two other teams: a team of stunt men and a team of martial-arts specialists for the action scenes.

Except for a tiny microphone inside the head and two eyeholes, an actor playing a Turtle was really cut off from the outside world. The film was shot in the summertime, mostly in North Carolina, where summers are hot and humid. Wearing the costume was extremely uncomfortable. Actor Michelan Sisti, who played Michaelangelo, lost 15 pounds in two weeks.

The Turtles' facial expressions were controlled electronically. Expert puppeteers used radio control and computer technology to change their

Michael Turney, who played Danny, has a look of innocence. It makes his character more complex.

With all this fancy equipment, the Turtles became solid, three-dimensional versions of the comic-book and cartoon Turtles. They came to life even more because they had a glint in their eyes. A tiny light was made to be reflected in their eyes, making them look alive.

For the plot of the movie, some of the best sequences from the comics were woven together into a new story. The history of Splinter and the Turtles is the version from the comics. The incident of April's apartment being trashed is taken from the comics. So is the following scene in which April and the Turtles move to the country for some

facial expressions and move their lips. Working the Turtles was similar to playing a Nintendo game, because the puppeteers used joysticks. Each puppeteer was in charge of 30 motorized cables in each Turtle's head. These cables corresponded to 17 separate movements between the eyebrows and the jaw.

Once the sparkle was added to the Turtles' eyes, they really came to life.

The fight scenes, like the one on April's rooftop, were carefully choreographed—much like a complex dance routine.

peace. The movie is very much like a comic-book adventure.

The movie's director, Steve Barron, told the *Chicago Tribune* that "kids pick up on the satire" of the movie "and the concept that a turtle, which is the slowest animal, could be the fastest." The movie is not simply a spoof of superhuman comic-book heroes, which is what the creators originally intended. It's an appeal not to judge a book by its cover. In this way, the movie preaches tolerance and acceptance of those of us who are different.

Most of the humans in the movie are prejudiced against the Turtles because the Turtles aren't like them. The Turtles are seen not for the good they do, but for their looks. Teens are sympathetic to this, because they can be misunderstood in the same way. And kids like the close relationship the Turtles have with their father figure, Splinter.

Some people object to the violence in the movie. But the green teens, after all, don't like to engage in battle unless they are attacked first, or if they see that someone else is in danger. They believe in "live and let live."

Boys like the film because it portrays friendship between boys in a good light. Young boys prize teamwork and the bond of friendship. The Turtles are examples of the kind of group spirit that boys like. Kids also like the fact that the Turtles speak a slang language that adults don't understand.

But most important, kids like the film because it's adventure-filled, hip, and fun. They come out of the movie theater energized. And the kids aren't the only ones who like the movie. A good many parents have been surprised to find themselves enjoying *Teenage Mutant Ninja Turtles*. Even though kids pay a reduced ticket price, it's now the most successful independent film—that is, one that wasn't made by one of the big studios—in history.

Toshishiro Obata, who played Tatsu, has black-belt degrees in at least eight martial arts.

TURTLES VIDEO & VINYL

Hot Rodding Teenagers

Fun-loving teenagers from Dimension X, the Neutrinos, escape their battle-torn planet and arrive on Earth. The Shredder's Stone Warriors pursue them, but the Turtles come to their aid. At the same time, the Shredder and Krang want to unleash chaos on the world. The Turtles have to prevent that, too. This is an especially challenging mission, because the evil ones have a weather machine that can destroy life on the planet.

This video also includes *A Thing About Rats.* The Shredder understands that to defeat the Turtles he needs to get rid of Splinter. He sends an army of mousers—mechanical rat-catchers invented by Baxter Stockman. But his plot is foiled by Splinter and the Turtles.

Cowabunga, Shredhead

In this story, the Shredder makes hologram look-alikes of his enemies. He intends to have the holograms take the place of the originals and become his puppets. First on his list is Michaelangelo. But Mike's hologram malfunctions. It behaves like Mike, but it looks like the Shredder himself! There's plenty of confusion for our green teens to overcome in this tale about the difference between illusion and reality.

This video also includes *New York's Shiniest.* A robot invented by the police to fight crime is duplicated by the Shredder, who now has an army of such robots. But with April's gusto and the brave spirit of the Turtles, the evil ones meet their match.

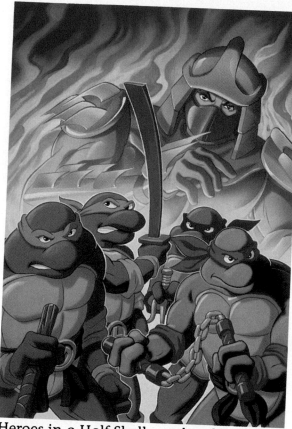

Heroes in a Half Shell, *produced by Murakami Wolf Swenson, Inc., was the first of the cartoon videos.*

Heroes in a Half Shell

This is the first video adventure of the green teens, and it introduces April to the Turtles and Splinter. In this story, the Shredder creates his two stupid baddies, Rocksteady and Bebop.

The Shredder is Splintered

The Shredder has a "retromutagen" ray gun that can undo mutants. Splinter would like to use this ray gun so that he can be his old ninja human self again. But the Shredder refuses to help out and, instead, provides Krang with a huge body. This tale proposes the theory that the mind is everlasting, but the body is only temporary and can be changed for better or worse.

The Return of the Shredder is also included in this video. The evil one returns from Dimension X to fight the Turtles once again. This time, Krang orders him to fend for himself without sophisticated weapons. The Shredder trains martial-arts students to impersonate the Turtles and commit crimes in their name. But our fearsome foursome fight back!

Case of the Killer Pizzas

In this one, Krang invents—and the Shredder unleashes—meatball-shaped eggs that, when microwaved, hatch into monsters. The plan is to put them on pizzas and lure the Turtles to this deadly version of their favorite food. But Splinter is onto the trap. Unfortunately, the microwaved creatures escape into the sewers, where they grow into huge, yellow monsters. Fortunately, Leonardo figures out a way to defeat them.

This video also includes *Return of the Fly,* in which the Shredder cross-mutates Baxter with a fly. Like the hero in the movie *The Fly,* Baxter turns into a large, bizarre fly.

Our heroes must look like snacks to Bebop and Rocksteady!

Super Rocksteady and Mighty Bebop

The two clumsy mutants, Rocksteady and Bebop, try to hypnotize the whole city with a mind-controlling mesmerizer. Naturally, they goof up the job. They are punished by being cross-mutated with a computer into super versions of themselves. But the Turtles prove themselves equal to this challenge. The story's point is that having an independent mind is better than following the crowd.

The Mutagen Monster is also included in this video. Toxic goo transforms a cow into a mad bull that goes wild. The Shredder wants to use the bull to fight the Turtles, but our green teens manage to prevent the beast from terrorizing the city.

Incredible Shrinking Turtles

This is a four-part feature-length adventure of the Turtles. One part is a Turtles variation of the movies *The Incredible*

Shrinking Man and *Honey, I Shrunk the Kids.* The Shredder and the Turtles are after three fragments of an alien ship that would give them unlimited power. With one fragment, the Shredder shrinks our heroes, who must endure terrible danger because of their tiny size. Will April and Splinter help them grow back?

In part two, the Shredder returns from Dimension X to find the second alien fragment. But the fragment causes a speck of dust on the Shredder's boot to grow into a huge mutant plant. The city is almost choked by the plant—until the Turtles arrive.

Part three shows the Shredder finding another alien fragment, which he hooks up to the city's electrical power. That gives him control over every single machine in the city. But the Turtles find a way out.

In the final chapter, the Shredder discovers that together, all three fragments form an "evil eye." The race for this evil eye is on, as the two camps find and lose it.

VINYL

The soundtrack of the movie *Teenage Mutant Ninja Turtles* is mostly upbeat, funky rap music. The lyrics try to make a positive comment about society and young people's behavior. These are the eleven songs:

"This Is What We Do," by
    M.C. Hammer
"Spin That Wheel," by
    Hi Tek 3
"Family," by Riff
"9.95," by Spunkadelic
"Turtle Power," by
    Partners in Kryme
"Let the Walls Come Down,"
    by Johnny Kemp
"Every Heart Needs a Home,"
    by St. Paul
"Shredder's Suite," by
    John Du Prez
"Splinter's Tale I" and
    "Splinter's Tale II," by
    John Du Prez
"Turtle Rhapsody," by
    Orchestra on the Half Shell

TURTLES EVERYWHERE

ike many characters in kids' TV shows, the Teenage Mutant Ninja Turtles appear on licensed toys and products of all descriptions. Turtlesmania has become a $500-million-a-year business, with 175 licensed manufacturers turning out 1000 different products. In 1989, the Turtles action figures were the toy industry's third-hottest-selling line, behind Barbie and Nintendo.

Mark Freedman is the man behind all this merchandising. He heard about the Turtles, and when he met Kevin Eastman and Peter Laird, the Turtles' creators, he thought the Turtles would make a good line of toys. Action figures tended to be all the same—heroes with high-tech weapons. He thought that the idea of turtles mutating into teenagers and being trained as ninjas was so wild, the toys would stand out from the rest.

Freedman took his idea to Playmates Toys, Inc. He knew that this was a toy company that wanted to produce an action figure that was less military than G.I. Joe and the Masters of the Universe. Playmates liked the concept of the Turtles because they were funny.

At first, the reaction from buyers at toy stores was less

Playmates Toys, Inc., has crafted their line of TMNT action figures with great detail.

than enthusiastic. Many of them thought the color green was a turnoff; it wouldn't sell. But by mid-1990, probably 50 million Turtles action figures had been sold.

So far, 30 action figures have been crafted, and the number is climbing all the time. Mike, Don, Leo, and Raph each carries his characteristic weapons. Splinter, their mentor, comes with a bow and arrow. April O'Neil—the figure that is the hardest to find—wears her yellow jumpsuit, and she comes complete with a video camera. Casey Jones carries his hockey stick and his bats in a bag around his neck.

You can also have the Shredder, in his mask and cape, and if you've got several of the Foot Soldiers, you can furnish him with an army. The bodiless Krang comes as a pink blobby brain perched on a mechanical body. Bebop and Rocksteady both carry manhole covers and laser guns and blasters. Baxter

Stockman appears in his role as a mutated fly. The entire cast of characters includes many others—*samurai* rabbit Usagi Yojimbo, Ace Duck, the Rat King, to name a few—and new characters are in the works.

To help bring your Turtles action figures to life, you can add a Turtle Blimp with detachable glider, a miniature sewer system modeled after the Turtles' home, and various Turtles vehicles. You can even buy Retromutagen Ooze—a green, gooey substance that represents the stuff that transformed the Turtles. A tiny "premutant" plastic turtle is included.

Some stores have reported that sales have almost doubled since the Turtles movie came out. More than a few toy stores were not ready for Turtlesmania and found themselves running out of merchandise to sell. Distributors of movie products say that the craze for Ninja Turtles is so

The Turtle Blimp is one of several action vehicles created by Playmates Toys, Inc. When held aloft, it can drop its "bombs" on the enemy.

strong, they can sell anything Turtles-related.

And the action figures are only part of the story. The fun and games continue with computer games, board games, and trading cards. There are even Turtles greeting cards. Mello Smello, a company in New Hope, Minnesota, has a license to make scratch-and-sniff stickers. The odor that results is,

The Sewer Playset by Playmates Toys, Inc., is a kid's dream toy—complete with a working elevator!

of course, pepperoni pizza. The company reports that their Turtles scratch-and-sniff stickers have sold faster than any of the company's other lines.

Turtles fans can literally fill their day with pleasures that have to do with our green heroes. In the morning, when you wake up, there's a marshmallow-strewn Turtles breakfast cereal. You can drink your milk or juice with a Turtles drinking straw, sample a Turtles yogurt, and eat off a Turtles plate.

Later in the day, you can have Turtles pork rinds, Turtles fruit drinks, and Turtles candy, ice cream, and cookies—all bearing the mark of the green teens. You can carry them in your Turtles lunch box.

And you can get a Turtles frozen pizza—no anchovies, of course. Since one brand of frozen pizza started carrying the Turtles on the box, sales have doubled—even though it's exactly the same pizza at the same price as it was without the Turtles.

Lounge in total Turtles style with a Turtles T-shirt and plush slippers adorned with a Turtle face.

After eating these Turtles-supported foods, you could brush your teeth with a Turtles musical toothbrush that actually reminds you to brush after every meal!

How about getting dressed with reptilian style, dudes? Like any fad, the Turtles have their own T-shirts. For something

A fan can wear Turtles from head to toe. These skates sure make a radical sidewalk statement!

different, try on Turtles boxer shorts, jogging suits, socks, belts, shoes, or sneakers. In rainy weather, keep your shell dry with a Turtles raincoat.

Top it all off with a Turtles baseball cap. Then you're probably ready to hop on your Turtles skateboard or try out your Turtles roller skates.

At school, you can take notes in your Turtles notebook, find the date on your Turtles calendar, and solve math problems on your Turtles calculator. Check the time on your Turtles watch, and make sure your keys are not lost by keeping them on a Turtles key chain.

After a hard ninja day, you could take a shower using Turtles soap, wash your hair in Turtles shampoo, or dip your shell in a Turtles bubble bath. Slip into your Turtles bedroom slippers. You'll be ready for a good night's sleep in your Turtles pajamas between your Turtles sheets. Even your night light can have the Turtles watching over you.

What do you think is inside this Turtles-ized gift? It could be one of the many TMNT products on the market.

On a camping trip or in your backyard, you can use sleeping bags, slumber tents, backpacks, and water bottles that carry the image of the green teens. In case of a cut, you can cover it with a Turtles bandage.

And there is more: yo-yos, magnets, decals, posters, balloons, badges, coloring books, puzzles—even Turtles commemorative coins. If you buy any of these as a gift for someone, you can wrap it in Turtles gift wrap.

This bonanza of Turtles merchandise in the stores has kids begging for more and parents wondering when to say no. But some products have been refused a license. The merchandisers of Turtles items would not allow the green teens' name to be attached to something that has no meaning to our reptilian heroes. A Turtles cologne was turned down, as was a Turtles fishing pole. Can you imagine the Turtles giving their hand to capturing fish from the same type of pond where they themselves were born?

Though it's possible that Turtlesmania will fade in time, Mark Freedman hopes that the Turtles will be a marketing staple, like the Disney cartoon characters Mickey Mouse and Donald Duck. It seems that every kid in America is wild about the Turtles, but their overseas popularity is just beginning. The Turtles cartoons have only recently started running in Australia, New Zealand, and parts of Europe. In Great Britain, the Turtles are already popular. Perhaps the Teenage Mutant Ninja Turtles will find worldwide fame.

NINTENDO TURTLES

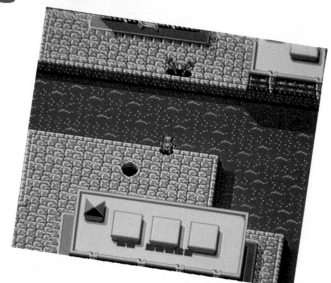

 ur favorite green teens are now the subjects of a Nintendo video game. *Teenage Mutant Ninja Turtles*, the video game, has the same name, look, and kooky sense of humor as the comics and the movie—as well as Raphael, Donatello, Leonardo, and Michaelangelo. You go through several "areas," each holding a different challenge. In Area 1, the Shredder's Foot Clan has kidnapped April and taken her to a hideout in a building. You take the part of any of the four Turtles and try to rescue April.

You start the action in Area 1, with a bird's-eye view of the streets of New York City. You immediately check out the scene for an open manhole cover down into the sewers, like the one near the center of this picture. Here in Area 1, move in a counterclockwise direction, from the open manhole to the right, then up, and then to the left.

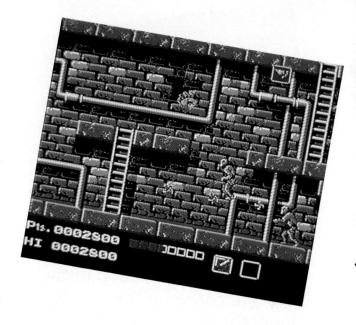

The information screen shows your current position on the ground. You also call up this screen when you want to change Turtles. Whenever one of your Turtles is injured, you should switch to another Ninja Turtle. That way, you won't have to start all over at the beginning of a level when a Turtle is captured.

Hint: If you come across a pizza, and you're not under direct attack at the moment, switch to your weakest Turtle and feed him to restore his health.

Down in the sewer beneath Area 1, you run into many of the Turtles' enemies, all armed and dangerous. Use the full length, width, height, and depth of each screen, and don't forget to use your Turtle's special ninja abilities. In this scene, Michaelangelo is using his *nunchukus* to fight against a Foot Clan soldier. To escape the throwing stars they have launched at him, he jumps up into the air and rolls himself into a ball.

Hint: The slice of pizza in the upper right corner is worth a bite, if you can get over there.

At the end of Area 1, the kidnapped April is guarded by Shredder's cohort Bebop at the top right corner of the screen. Donatello and his *bo* stick is the best Ninja Turtle to do battle with him.

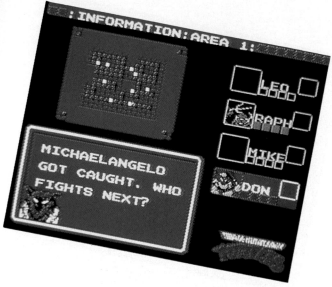

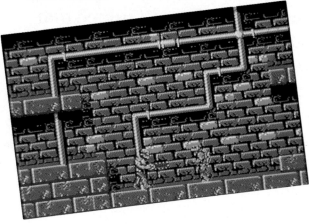

Some of the bad guys don't fight fair. This creep is carrying a chain saw, so don't get anywhere near him. Use a Turtle with a long reach—either Leonardo and his *katana* sword or Donatello and his *bo* stick.

Any time one of the Turtles is captured, you're returned to the information screen and asked to select a new fighter. Both Leonardo and Michaelangelo have been removed from the scene, so your choice is limited to the two remaining Turtles. One of the keys to winning this game is to avoid having to face such a choice. You should change to another Turtle before one of your team members is completely exhausted.

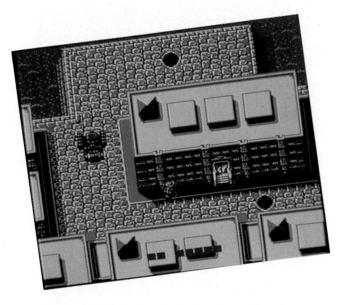

Leonardo is wielding his *katana* sword in the final stages of Area 1. Roof Leapers are pouncing from above and one-way conveyor belts always seem to be going the wrong way. Jump against the direction of the arrows and keep moving to go in the direction you want.

Sometimes you have to deal with the assaults of Foot Clan platoons in Roller Cars like the one just left of center. There's not a whole lot you can do about the Roller Cars except to try to avoid them. Jump onto the sidewalks if you can, or go down into the nearest manhole. You can always climb back up and out of the manhole in a few seconds and then continue on your way.

April is being held in a warehouse by Bebop. He's got a machine gun, so call on Don or Leo—they can keep a safe distance and still put up a good fight.

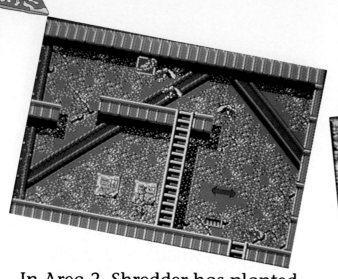

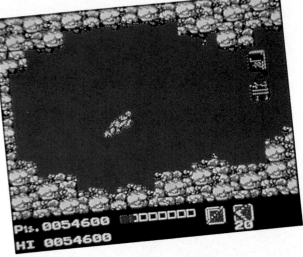

In Area 2, Shredder has planted eight bombs under a dam. If they explode, the whole city will be flooded. You have only two minutes and twenty seconds to find and disarm them.

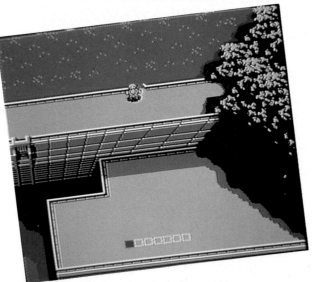

Once you've fought your way to the top of the dam, locate the notch in the wall and dive off into the water, then try to disarm the devices.

While you're underwater, you have to be careful not to confuse a bomb with a trap. But don't waste any time, because the clock is ticking. Here is one successful route: After you've defused the first bomb, stay along the bottom channel and go for the second. Then double back to the left and go up for number three and then right for four and five. Come back a little way, then go up and to the right for the sixth bomb. Double back, then go down and to your right (the Turtle's left) for number seven. You can find the last bomb by going down, to the right, and back to the left.

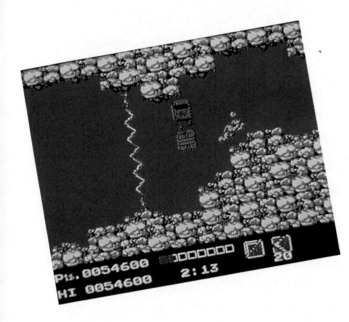

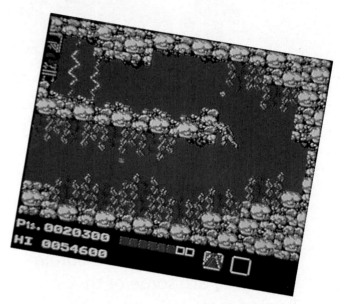

Avoiding the electromagnetic barriers is a matter of timing—wait to cross between the pulses. But if you are almost out of time, it might make sense simply to blunder on through the barriers. Just be careful not to deplete the power of one of your Turtles. If you do, you have to start this area all over again.

The final bomb of Area 2 is located at the end of this double-back. The seaweed will give you a nasty sting and the electrical barrier is two pulses wide, but who ever said being a Teenage Mutant Ninja Turtle was easy? When you go on to Area 3, you'll have to rescue Master Splinter. He's been kidnapped. In this area, you get wheels of your own, the Party Wagon, armed with missiles to blow up barricades.

TURTLESPEAK

Part of the charm of the Teenage Mutant Ninja Turtles is that they sound like kids—*California* kids. Here are some of the Turtles' favorite expressions:

Peel rubber: This is a drag-racing expression, meaning that a start was so fast, the tires left rubber tracks on the road! When the Turtles say, "Let's peel rubber," you know they're not going to hang around much longer.

Cowabunga: This is the Turtles' battle cry. It can be an expression of excitement, or it can be used as encouragement in a fight. "Cowabunga" originally came from the old Howdy Doody TV show. The word has come to be associated most closely with Mike. When he swings into action his call is "Cowabunga!" When the sewers are flooded, and the Turtles must swim for their lives, Mike yells, "Cowabunga!" to give them heart.

Radical: This adjective means extremely good. It's what the Turtles say when they are excited by something or someone. "Radical" is a little different from "awesome," another of their favorite words. They use "awesome" to express wonder and astonishment.

Dude: In tortoise jargon, this word means "guy." Originally, "dude" meant a dandy, a man conceited about his clothes. But in Turtlese, it is an informal, friendly word that can be a greeting. "Hey, dude!" The Turtles are, after all, hip dudes.

Four tubular dudes chow down on a rad pizza and ride an awesome wave! Cowabunga!

Mondo: This is a Spanish and Italian adjective meaning "pure." The Turtles use it to strengthen the meaning of the word that follows, like "very" in English. They might say someone is "mondo brave."

Tubular: This word is another adjective that expresses approval. The more intense form is "tubuloso," in the same way that "fabuloso" is a more intense form of "fabulous."

Scope out: This expression means "take a look at" or "check it out." When the green teens meet the Rock Soldiers from Dimension X, they can't help saying, "Scope out those awesome outfits!"

No problemo: The Turtles are confident they can handle most situations. If they size up a problem as being fixable, they'll say, "No problemo!"

Maximum wipe-out: This is how the Turtles would describe a complete defeat of the enemy after an intense ninja face-off. "It's a maximum wipe-out!" they'd cry with excitement. They can also say "totally trashed" or "totally totaled."

Mega-move: This is what the Turtles would call a grand or clever action. A terrific plan put into action is a "mega-move."

The ultimo bummer: A situation that is disappointing is a "bummer," but a situation that is extremely unsatisfactory is "the ultimo bummer." When the Turtles get trapped by the Shredder, or if they miss out on an opportunity to fight evil, they say: "The ultimo bummer, dudes!"

TURTLE MAZE

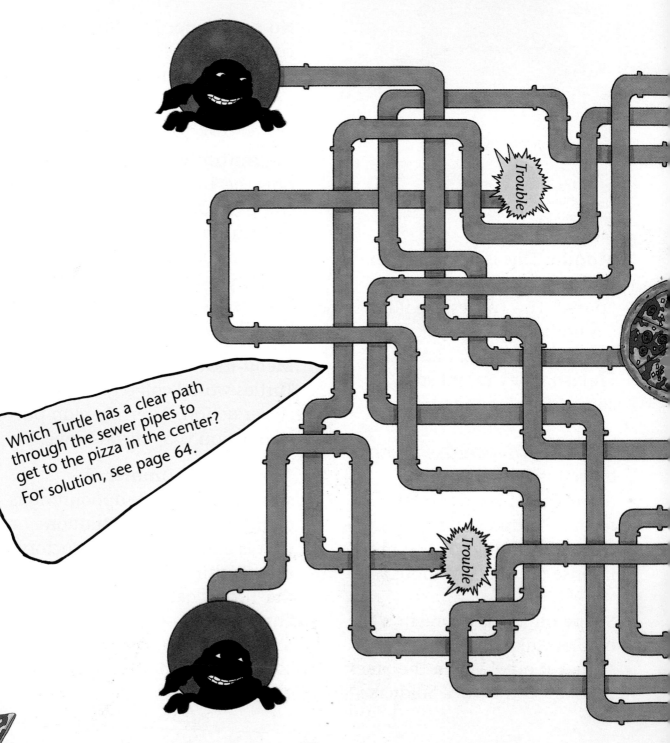

Which Turtle has a clear path through the sewer pipes to get to the pizza in the center? For solution, see page 64.

KNOW YOUR TURTLES

In 1991, the Shredder will team up with an evil turtle called Flash.

Leonardo's *katana* blade is a long sword that is traditionally used by the Japanese ninjas.

For breakfast, Splinter prefers *sushi* to pizza.

April was named after the girlfriend of Kevin Eastman, one of the creators of the Turtles.

Splinter comes from Japan, so he eats sushi for breakfast.

Mike's favorite weapons, the *nunchukus*, are also known as nunchucks or simply chucks.

Of the four Turtles, Raphael is the one who jumps first and looks later. He does learn from his mistakes, though.

In the movie, Donatello's voice was that of Corey Feldman.

Michaelangelo calls himself "the master of the whirling pizzas."

Splinter and the Turtles live in the sewers, but they have made a home for themselves with love and respect for one another.

You didn't see actor Corey Feldman in the movie Teenage Mutant Ninja Turtles, but he contributed—he's the voice of Donatello.

Splinter teaches the Turtles to avoid trouble if possible. They will not fight unless they really have to.

Leonardo is the oldest Turtle of the bunch. He's 16, but that's people years, not turtle years.

Splinter helps the Turtles adjust to the real world by teaching them not only how to fight, but also how to keep cool and collected.

Raphael is also known as the "Snapping Ninja."

TURTLES TRIVIA QUIZ

1. Where do the Turtles live?
2. How did they get their names?
3. Who is the unofficial leader of the group?
4. Which Turtle is the jokester?
5. Which Turtle is the master handyman who can fix anything?
6. Who is the most intense of the four Turtles?
7. What kind of animal is Splinter?
8. Who is Splinter's enemy, the evil ninja who wants to control the world?
9. What do the Turtles hate to have on their pizzas?
10. Which Turtle does a James Cagney imitation?
11. In the movie, which Turtle has the voice of Corey Feldman?
12. Which of the Turtles uses the ninja weapon *sai*?
13. In the movie, when Splinter is taken by the Shredder, which Turtle was able to concentrate and hear his master's voice?
14. Which of the Turtles' friends used to be a professional hockey player?
15. What is the name of the Turtles' housekeeper?

ANSWERS

1. The sewers of New York City 2. Splinter named them after famous Italian artists 3. Leonardo 4. Michaelangelo 5. Donatello 6. Raphael 7. A rat 8. The Shredder 9. Anchovies 10. Michaelangelo 11. Donatello 12. Raphael 13. Leonardo 14. Casey Jones 15. Metalhead. Answer to Turtles Maze, pages 60-61: The Turtle in the lower left-hand corner.